SOLIHULL LIBRARY SERVICE

This book must be returned to any Solihull library on or before the latest date stamped on the label. It may be renewed up to three times unless another reader has reserved it.

You may renew by telephoning your local branch during library opening hours.

Details of charges, loan periods and other matters may be seen in the library or visit our website: www.solihull.gov.uk/wwwlib/

BORROWERS are responsible for any damage to items while in their possession.
L.3a

THE
SAXONS AND VIKINGS
RECONSTRUCTED

Jason Hook
Photographs by Martyn F. Chillmaid

HODDER
Wayland
An imprint of Hodder Children's Books

RECONSTRUCTED

Other titles in this series:
The Home Front • The Romans
The Tudors • The Victorians

Conceived and produced for Hodder Wayland by

Nutshell
MEDIA

Intergen House, 65–67 Western Road, Hove BN3 2JQ, UK
www.nutshellmedialtd.co.uk

Editor: Polly Goodman
Designer: Simon Borrough
All reconstructions set-up and photographed by: Martyn F. Chillmaid

First published in Great Britain in 2003 by Hodder Wayland,
an imprint of Hodder Children's Books.

Hook, Jason
The Saxons & Vikings. – (Reconstructed)
1. Saxons – Social life and customs – Pictorial works – Juvenile literature
2. Vikings – Social life and customs – Pictorial works – Juvenile literature
I. Title
942'.017'0222

ISBN 0 7502 4311 2

Printed and bound in Hong Kong.

Hodder Children's Books
A division of Hodder Headline Limited
338 Euston Road, London NW1 3BH

Cover photographs: main photo: A Saxon warrior prepares to defend his home against Viking
raiders; from top to bottom: a Saxon villager outside her house; a selection of Saxon and Viking
food; women prepare a meal in a Saxon hall; a Saxon court; Saxon warriors prepare to fight.

Title page: A comfortable Saxon village home.

Contents

Raiders

In the tenth century, England was a curious mixture of Saxon and Viking cultures. The Saxons had occupied the country since the fifth century, when they invaded England from Europe. Over the next few hundred years they worked hard clearing forests, and building villages and farms.

The Vikings, brilliant sailors and fierce warriors from Scandinavia, had made the first of many bloodthirsty raids in AD 793. They rampaged through the countryside, slaughtering all those who stood in their way. Then Viking settlers had arrived, and by the tenth century there were many Viking towns in northern England.

The tenth century was a time when the Saxons and the Vikings left a lasting impression on the English way of life: in the settlements they built, the religions they followed, the stories they told, and the languages they spoke.

(Below) On the northern coasts of Britain, some Viking settlers built farmhouses with walls and roofs made out of turf.

(Right) A Saxon warrior prepares to defend his home against Viking raiders.

Helmet

Face guard

Chain mail vest

Shield

Sword

Knife sheath

A Viking Town

The cluttered yard of a house in York.

In the tenth century, the greatest of the Viking towns in northern England was York, which the Vikings called Jorvik. It had been captured by Danish Vikings in 866, and developed into a bustling marketplace.

A strong wall surrounded York, defending the town from raiders. Inside the walls lay a network of narrow streets, with names such as Coppergate and Micklegate, after the Viking word *gate* meaning 'street'. Narrow wooden houses with thatched roofs were packed close together, with baskets, cloth and yarn hanging from the eaves. Pigsties, wells, rubbish heaps and latrines were crammed into foul-smelling yards.

Bucket of water

Thatch

Goose

Hen

Wicker basket

Dyed yarn

Merchants sailed into York to trade foreign goods for local craftwork, while people from nearby villages came to buy items not available in the countryside. Facing on to the streets were shop fronts and workshops, where craftsmen such as leather-workers went about their work.

Leather was as widely used in Saxon and Viking times as plastic is today. The leather-worker laboured at a bench making belts, bags, purses, knife sheaths and other leather goods. He spent much of his time making boots, shoes, and even ice-skates. A wooden model of a foot, called a 'last', was used to hold the leather in shape as it was sewn into a shoe. Many people could not afford new shoes, but they still took their old ones to the leather-worker to be mended.

The workbench in a Viking leather-worker's shop.

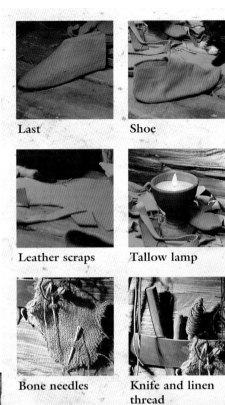

Last

Shoe

Leather scraps

Tallow lamp

Bone needles

Knife and linen thread

Craftworkers and Traders

All manner of craftworkers made and traded their goods in the workshops of York, and they all created work for each other. The leather-worker, for example, used cowhide and deerskin traded from a local tanner. To cut the shape of a shoe, he used a steel knife made and sharpened by a blacksmith. He stitched the shoes using a needle traded from a carver of bone and antler. And all the work was done in a workshop lit by a clay lamp made by a local potter.

Bucket   Stool   Cup   Bowls

Spoons   Spindles   Axe   Deer antler

Woodworking was a traditional skill of the Vikings, who were famous for their shipbuilding. At York, there were many stalls selling wooden stools, buckets, bowls, cups and spindles. Using a machine called a lathe, a woodworker could turn a piece of wood and shape it with a sharp tool.

A market stall selling wooden goods in York.

Carvers made many articles out of bones and deer antlers, including pins, combs and comb-cases with carved decorations. One Saxon writer, John of Wallingford, complained at the way the Vikings were always combing their hair. In York, traders looked for local specialities, such as jewellery, embroideries and silver. York had its own mint, where silver was hammered between two moulds to make coins. Merchants carried portable scales to weigh the silver coins. Sometimes they chopped coins into pieces, known as hacksilver, to make small change.

Viking merchants were fearless sailors who voyaged west as far as Greenland and east to Russia to meet traders from China and Arabia. When they arrived in York, they brought with them a magnificent variety of goods. There were animal furs and amber from the Baltic, human slaves from eastern Europe, walrus ivory and hides from the Arctic, and swords and mill stones from Denmark and Norway. Luxuries included silk from China, spices from Arabia, cowrie shells from the Red Sea, and the soft down of the eider duck for stuffing pillows. Some cunning Vikings even sold the spiral-shaped horn of the narwhal, a sea creature of the Arctic, claiming that it had been captured from a unicorn!

Goods carved from bone and antler.

Deer antler

Combs

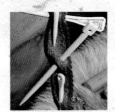

Bone pins

Horn buckles and bone needles

Houses and Homes

A comfortable house in a Saxon settlement.

Thatched roof

Ash rafter

Oak planks

Firewood

Buckets of water

Basket

In Saxon villages, farmers called *churls* lived in houses similar to those in Viking towns. Walls of oak planks were sealed with clay, and ash rafters supported a thatched roof. Unlike the neatly arranged houses of a Viking street, Saxon village houses were scattered about. At the centre of the village was the long hall. This was a much bigger house, which belonged to the local *thane*, or lord. Here, feasts and entertainments were often held.

Inside a Saxon or Viking house there was a single, gloomy room. There were no windows, and the only light came from lamps and a fire built in a hearth. The fire was the centre of the home, supplying light and heat for cooking. But there was no chimney, so everything in the room had the same smell – smoke!

A large family all worked, played and slept in the one room. Floorboards were built across a pit, so that the damp earth did not make them rot, and these must have drummed as children ran across them. To add to the smell and noise, cows and pigs sometimes slept in the house during winter.

A raised platform might be used for seating or a bed, with bracken laid down as a mattress. Many families had a lathe for woodworking and a loom for weaving cloth. Kitchen utensils included storage jugs and jars, knives and spoons, iron and clay pots for boiling food over the fire, and wooden boards that served as plates. There were no cupboards, so food was hung up in sacks out of the reach of rats.

The names of Saxon and Viking settlements are still in use today. Saxon village names include words such as *den* (pig pasture), *ham* (estate) and *leigh* (clearing): for example, Tenterden, Grantham and Oakleigh. Many northern towns have Viking names. These often include *by* (town) or *thorpe* (small settlement): for example, Whitby and Owsthorpe.

Food sack   Storage jar

Tallow lamp   Cooking pot

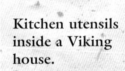

Spatulas   Drinking glasses

Kitchen utensils inside a Viking house.   Shears

Village Life

Everyone in a Saxon village had to work hard to survive, and children shared in the daily tasks from an early age. They helped to feed the pigs and chickens, milked the cows, goats and sheep, and collected honey from the family beehives.

Women and children wandered into the surrounding woods to gather supplies. These included firewood and water, moss for toilet paper, cotton grass for lamp wicks, herbs for cooking and medicine, berries and birds' eggs for food and, when grain was short, acorns for making a rough sort of bread.

Villages were surrounded by fields owned by the local *thane*, who allowed the *churls* to farm them. In return, the *churls* fought for the *thane*, worked up to three days a week on his land, and paid an annual rent such as a pig. Slaves called *thralls* had no land, but performed everyday tasks such as thatching roofs.

Thatching   Carrying water

Feeding chickens   Chopping wood

Saxon villagers go about their everyday tasks.

Saxon villagers used ploughs hauled by oxen to dig long, deep furrows into their fields. These furrows were measured in *furrowlongs*, which was the distance an oxen could drag the plough before resting. This is how the modern measure of a furlong got its name.

The villagers sowed their ploughed fields with crops such as barley, wheat, peas and beans. They also had fields of pasture for their animals. The Saxons were famous for the quality of the wool they produced, and shepherds guarded their precious flocks of sheep. This was vital because in Saxon times there were still wolves prowling the English countryside.

In the tenth century, travel was slow and dangerous, with outlaws stalking the roads. People did not travel regularly, so the arrival of strangers in the village was a special event. *Thanes*, priests and pilgrims sometimes came, but the most exciting visitors were the travelling pedlars and craftsmen. Pedlars sold important goods such as salt and iron tools, while wandering craftsmen included carpenters and leather-workers. In remote places, these travellers were the only source of news from around the country.

A travelling leather-worker mends a villager's shoe.

Shoe

Linen thread

Needle

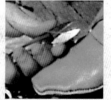

Scissor shears

Clothing

Saxon *churls* and a warrior catch up on the latest news, wearing clothes typical of the time.

The typical dress of a Saxon *churl* was a round-necked, long-sleeved woollen tunic, tied at the waist with a belt. Trousers, called *braies*, were worn tucked into stockings, or bound with garters known as *yorkies*. Cloaks were fastened at the right shoulder with a circular brooch, to leave the right arm free to draw a sword. 'Phrygian' caps of wool or leather were worn by some Saxon men. Saxon and Viking men often grew beards, and among fashionable Vikings these were parted into forks or plaits.

Women in tenth-century England wore a full-length woollen gown tied at the waist with a belt. Beneath the gown were undergowns, dyed in lighter colours. The top gown was called a *roc*, from which we get the word 'frock'. Women also wore cloaks, held by a fastening across the chest. Their shoes were similar to men's, but were dyed in brighter colours such as red or blue.

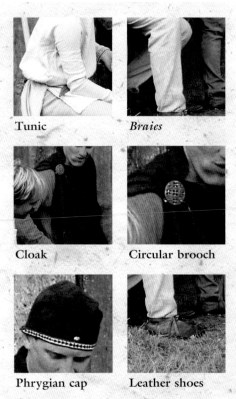

Tunic

Braies

Cloak

Circular brooch

Phrygian cap

Leather shoes

Women covered their heads with a headscarf for warmth, but they still used combs to brush their hair. They also plucked out hair with tweezers, and used nail files and toothpicks. Jewellery included necklaces, pendants, bracelets and rings. Brooches came in all shapes and sizes, from the popular circular varieties to some shaped like animals and birds. Gold brooches that have survived to this day, inlaid with glass and precious stones, reveal the delicate skills of Saxon jewellers.

Viking settlers brought their own style of jewellery from Scandinavia. They wore arm-rings decorated with fabulous loops and swirls. Some were decorated with 'gripping beasts', fantastic creatures that looked like a cross between a dragon and a weasel. Viking women also hung the household keys from the brooches they wore, to show that they were in charge of the home.

Although Saxon and Viking clothes were similar, they varied from place to place, from year to year, and between the different classes. In one surviving letter, a Saxon man is told off by his brother for dressing 'in Danish fashion'.

Gown and undergown

Embroidered sleeve

Belt

Headscarf

Necklace

Knife

Purse

Child's tunic

Women and children wearing typical Saxon clothes.

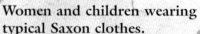

Food and Drink

Hearth   Cauldron

Wooden spoon   Clay bowls

Clay jug   Wooden bench

Women prepare a meal in a Saxon hall.

The Saxons ate many of the same vegetables that we eat today, though they would never have heard of a potato or a tomato. Fruits included apples, pears and medlars, which were similar to apples but only edible when they began to rot. There was no sugar, so honey was used to sweeten food.

Bread was baked on a stone set in the hearth. The bread the Saxons ate was made from rye and wheat, and was similar to modern wholemeal bread. Rye flat breads were also baked in the fire. Above the hearth, an iron cauldron was suspended from chains that reached up into the rafters. In this large pot, porridge and stews could be boiled up over the fire.

Beef, pork, lamb, oxen, chicken, geese and wildfowl were all eaten, although the only time poor people ate fresh meat was probably at community feasts. Sausages were made from horsemeat, lard and blood. Hares were hunted for their meat, but there were no rabbits in England at this time. In coastal villages, seabirds such as guillemots were snared.

There was not always enough fodder to keep animals alive through winter, and food could not be frozen. So finding other ways to preserve meat was important. It could be dried and packed in salt, hung from the rafters to be smoked by the constantly burning fire, or pickled in whey. Pickled meat had a rather sour taste, and salted or dried food might taste slightly rotten. So it was flavoured with mustard, horseradish and garlic.

Fish and shellfish were plentiful, and different regions had particular favourites. These included eels, crayfish, mussels, oysters and even shark. People were not fussy about which cut of meat they ate and all parts of an animal, including the head, would be boiled over the fire. Everyone carried a knife in their belt, and used this to tear the meat from whatever morsel was set before them.

A selection of Saxon and Viking food.

Dried fish

Whey

Flat breads

Salted cod

Sour milk

Sheep's head

Seabird eggs

Rye bread

Guillemot

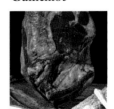
Smoked leg of lamb

Feasts

Feasting was a serious business in Saxon and Viking times. Feasts were held in villages to celebrate annual events, such as bringing in the harvest. In the long hall, trestle tables covered with linen cloth were set up for feasts. Shields and weapons were mounted on the walls, both as decoration and for the warriors to reach them quickly if an enemy attacked the village.

Among the Vikings, guests were welcomed to a feast by being handed towels and hot water. Saxon thanes handed out bread to their guests as they arrived. This symbolized their role in providing for the thralls, and the word 'lord' comes from a Saxon word meaning 'loaf guardian'.

A communal feast in the long hall.

Shield

Sword

Helmet

Trestle table

Jug of mead

Cup

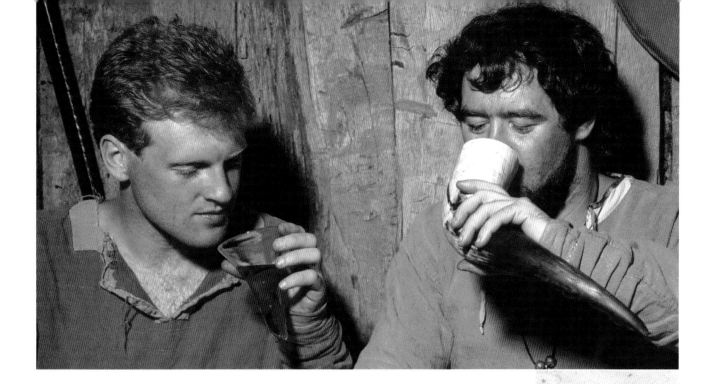

The favourite drinks at a feast were a mixture of fermented honey, called mead, and ale. Wealthy households used cone-shaped drinking vessels made from imported glass. But many people preferred traditional drinking horns, which were made from the horns of cattle. These magnificent horns were decorated with gold and silver engravings. Neither cone-shaped glasses nor drinking horns could be set down upright on a table, so when a drinking horn was filled it had to be emptied in one go. Feasts lasted throughout the night, and drunkenness was common.

Entertainment at a feast might include gambling with dice made out of animal bones. The Saxons enjoyed playing boardgames called 'Nine-man's Morris' and 'Fox and Geese'. The Vikings preferred games that were very similar to chess and draughts, as well as rougher pursuits. These included wrestling, and a swimming contest which involved half-drowning the opponent. Horse-fighting was also popular. Spectators placed bets on the outcome of a bloody fight between two stallions.

A very popular form of entertainment was the telling of riddles in verse, in which the listener had to solve a puzzle. One riddle went like this: 'I am solitary, wounded by iron / Battered by weapons, tired of battle / Weary of sword-edges.' The answer is a shield.

Saxon *churls* drink from glass and horn.

Drinking glass

Drinking horn

Storytelling

Another popular form of entertainment for the Saxons and the Vikings was the reciting of long poems by travelling storytellers. The poems told of great heroes, and taught the warriors how to be brave and generous. Most people in the tenth century could not write, so storytellers had to learn their tales by heart. In this way, stories were passed down from generation to generation without being written down.

The oldest surviving Saxon tale is called *Beowulf*. This epic poem tells of a Swedish prince, called Beowulf, who travels to the palace of the Danish King Hrothgar. Here, he defeats a bloodthirsty monster, named Grendel, who had been butchering warriors in the king's hall. *Beowulf* has over 3,000 lines and was recited from memory in long halls across the country for many years. It was finally written down by a monk in northern England around the tenth century, and survives to this day.

Viking storytellers told historical stories known as sagas. These used a type of verse called 'kenning', in which ordinary objects were given imaginative names. The sea, in one saga, is known as the 'whale's road', and blood is called 'wound dew'.

Although they feature fantastic monsters and amazing descriptions, Saxon and Viking tales were based on real events, and they often contain vital clues to help us reconstruct the past. One of the Viking stories, *The Saga of Eirik the Red*, tells how a Viking sailed west beyond Greenland to a mysterious country he called Vinland. Remains of a Viking settlement in Newfoundland have been found, proving that Vinland was in fact America and the saga records its discovery by the Vikings.

Clay hearth   Firewood   Plucked chicken   Log basket   Water bucket

A storyteller recites his story in a Saxon home.

Storyteller   Bed   Bed curtain

Law and Order

Law and order were very important to the Saxons and Vikings. The Saxons introduced the system of trial using a jury of twelve men. *Law*, *by-law* and *outlaw* are all Viking words. If a Viking or Saxon was killed in a fight, traditionally, his relatives would avenge him by killing his slayer. In this way, terrible feuds erupted between families, as one killing led to another. To stop this feuding, laws were introduced in Saxon times forcing a man to pay compensation to the family of the man he had killed. The amount depended on the dead man's rank, and was known as a person's *wergild*, or blood price. A *thane* might have a *wergild* of 1,200 shillings, while a *churl* was worth only 600. The poor *thralls* had no *wergild* at all.

A warrior offers compensation, or *wergild*, to the family of the man his brother killed.

Wergild

Chain mail shirt

Shield

Thane

Trials were held at a public meeting called a *moot* by the Saxons and a *thing* by the Vikings. The accused person had to swear their innocence, supported by oaths from their family. If the *moot* did not decide in their favour, a trial by 'ordeal' might take place. This took various forms. The accused might have to carry a red-hot iron bar, or pluck a stone from a cauldron of boiling water. Their hand would then be bandaged for three days. If the wound was still festering when the bandage was unwrapped, they would be found guilty.

Punishments could be brutal. Banishment of the guilty person from their family and home was a common sentence. Suspected witches were stoned to death or drowned. Bandits were flogged, had their little fingers cut off, or were scalped. Thieves, arsonists and murderers might all be sentenced to death by hanging. Gallows were set up at the boundaries between settlements. A Saxon poem, *The Fates of Men*, describes their use: 'One man must ride on the broad gallows, swing in death until the casket of his soul, his bleeding corpse, is torn to shreds as the dark-coated raven steals his eyes.'

Thane   *Churl*

Table   Guard

At a Saxon court, a *thane* passes sentence on a convicted *churl*.

War

Saxon warriors prepare for battle.

Spear

Shield

Boss

Helmet

Leather hat

When Saxon warriors invaded Britain's shores in the fifth century, they were greatly feared by the Britons. But when the Vikings made their first major raid, on Lindisfarne monastery in 793, it was the turn of the Saxons to feel dread and terror. The Vikings arrived suddenly in longships, with prows carved in the shape of dragons' heads, and fought with terrible savagery.

Warfare and violence were a way of life in Saxon times. By the tenth century, Saxon kings demanded that every settlement provide a certain number of men for the king's *fyrd*, or army, to help meet the Viking threat. If a *churl* refused to fight, and did not send someone in his place, his land was confiscated.

Most Saxons fought with spears and shields, but wealthier warriors carried swords. Blades were engraved with characters, called runes, which were believed to have magical powers. Some warriors also gave their swords names. Beowulf called his sword 'Roarer', perhaps because of the noise it made in battle. Some warriors were given chain mail shirts and iron helmets by their *thanes*. Shields of lime-wood and leather had an iron 'boss' to protect the hand, and were decorated with swirling lines.

Saxon and Viking warriors fought on foot, not on horseback. Armies formed walls of shields to defend themselves, and also used a wedge-shaped formation, which the Vikings called the 'gathering of pigs'!

The reign of terror enjoyed by the Vikings for hundreds of years was based on their savage brutality. In one incident, they murdered an archbishop by bombarding him with animal bones. Before battle, they sometimes unfurled a banner they called 'Land-waster'. This showed a raven, to remind their opponents that ravens would soon be pecking at their corpses. Then there was the 'blood eagle', a terrifying ritual in which Vikings pulled a prisoner's lungs out through his rib-cage to rest pulsing on his shoulders like an eagle's wings.

A Saxon warrior wearing a helmet with a face guard.

Sword

Helmet

Face guard

Chain mail shirt

Religion

When the Saxons first invaded Britain they were pagans. They worshipped a variety of fierce gods and nature spirits, and sacrificed animals in woodland shrines to appeal to the gods for successful harvests. Kings were buried inside entire ships loaded with goods, which, it was believed, they would carry to the afterlife.

The Saxons and Vikings worshipped similar pagan gods, including Thunor, or Thor, god of thunder. Storytellers told how Thor fought giants and dragons with a magical hammer. Warriors wore hammer-shaped amulets to appeal for the same strength. Other gods included Tiw, god of war, and Frigg, a fertility goddess. Then there was Woden, god of the dead. Warriors who died bravely in battle were carried by female spirits called Valkyries to Woden's hall in Valhalla. There, they spent their days in glorious battle and their nights feasting.

A bronze carving of Thor, the god of thunder, holding his magic hammer.

Magic hammer

Helmet

By the tenth century, however, most Saxons and Vikings were following the Christian religion. St Augustine, a prior from Rome, had converted the Saxon King Ethelbert in Canterbury, Kent, in 597, and the new faith had spread across the country like wildfire.

The conversion from paganism to Christianity was gradual, and at first the two religions were muddled. Some warriors carried a hammer of Thor and a Christian cross, which looked similar. Stone crosses were erected decorated with pagan runes, and churches were built on sites that had once been pagan shrines.

Christian celebrations gradually replaced pagan festivals, but they were held on the same dates. Easter took over the spring festival of the pagan goddess Eostre. Christmas replaced Yule, the midwinter feast at which the last of the year's fresh food was eaten.

The conversion of the Saxons and Vikings to Christianity created a way of life that lasted for thousands of years in Britain, with a farming village based around a central church. But the pagan gods have never been forgotten. Every week, on Tuesday (Tiw's Day), Wednesday (Woden's Day), Thursday (Thor's Day) and Friday (Frigg's Day), we reconstruct words that were first used in the world of the Saxons and Vikings.

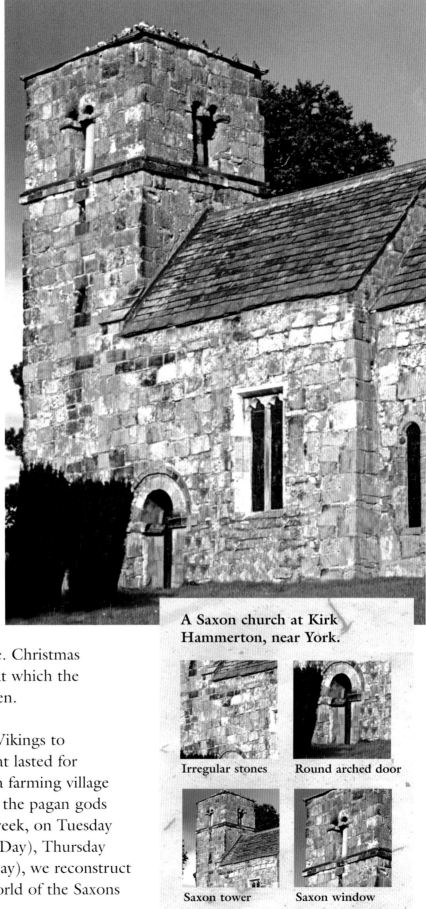

A Saxon church at Kirk Hammerton, near York.

Irregular stones

Round arched door

Saxon tower

Saxon window

Timeline

c.400 Saxon invaders begin the conquest of England.

410 The Roman emperor Honorius tells the Britons that the Romans can no longer defend them against invading tribes.

597 St Augustine lands in Kent, and converts the Saxon King Ethelbert to Christianity.

600 England is now divided into Saxon kingdoms.

c.625 A Saxon king is buried with his ship at Sutton Hoo, in Suffolk.

700 The epic poem *Beowulf* is written.

731 A monk called the Venerable Bede completes a book called *Ecclesiastical History of the English Nation*, which describes Saxon and Viking history.

760 King Offa, ruler of the Saxon kingdom of Mercia, introduces a silver English penny.

780 King Offa uses his sword-point to mark a boundary between England and Wales, on which he builds an earth bank known as Offa's Dyke.

787 Vikings make a small raid against Wareham, Dorset.

793 The Vikings make their first great raid, at the monastery on Lindisfarne, an island off the coast of Northumbria.

842 The Vikings attack London.

c.867 The 'Great Danish Army' of Vikings invades Northumbria.

871 King Alfred becomes ruler of the Saxon kingdom of Wessex, at a time when the Viking raids are at their most savage.

878 The Saxon King Alfred the Great defeats the Vikings at the Battle of Edington, in Wiltshire.

886 A treaty grants the Vikings the north-eastern region of England, which is known as the Danelaw.

c.890 Under King Alfred's rule, a book called *The Anglo-Saxon Chronicle* records the important events in England's history.

946 King Eadred becomes the Saxon King of England. He drives the Viking ruler of York, Eirik Bloody-Axe, out of the city.

1000 The Viking Leif Ericsson discovers America.

1016 The Danish Viking Canute becomes King of England. England is ruled by Viking kings until 1042.

1042 Edward the Confessor, a descendant of King Alfred, rules over England until 1066.

1066 The invasion of the Normans brings the era of the Saxons and Vikings in England to an end.

Note: The letter '*c*' is short for *circa*, which is the Latin word meaning 'approximately'.

Glossary

amber A precious yellow resin, used to make jewellery.

amulet A piece of jewellery believed to grant the wearer protection or good luck.

arsonists People who deliberately start fires.

banishment To be sent out of a settlement or country and forbidden to return.

boss The strong dome-shaped point at the centre of a shield, made of iron.

churls Saxon farmers, who worked on land owned by a *thane*.

embroideries Cloths decorated with needlework patterns.

epic A long poem, such as *Beowulf*, describing a hero's adventures or a country's history.

fodder Food for cattle and other animals.

furlong A measurement of distance equal to 220 yards or 201 metres.

gallows A structure used for hanging people.

hides Animal skins.

imported Brought in to one country from another.

ivory A precious hard, white material made from animals' tusks or teeth.

lathe A machine used for shaping wooden objects.

latrines Simple pits, used as toilets.

linen Cloth made from a type of plant called flax.

longships The fast sailing ships of the Vikings.

loom A machine used for weaving thread into cloth.

mail A material made from chains of iron links.

mill stones Stones used in a mill for grinding grain into flour.

mint A place where money is made.

pagans People who hold religious beliefs that do not belong to the world's main religions. The Saxons and Vikings were pagans because they worshipped a variety of gods and nature spirits.

pedlars Wandering traders.

pilgrims People who make journeys for religious reasons, for example to visit a holy place.

runes Characters in an alphabet used in Saxon and Viking times.

sagas Long stories about heroic adventures, particularly those of the Vikings.

shrines Places where religious ceremonies take place.

stallions Adult male horses.

tallow Animal fat used in candles and soap.

tanner A worker who treats animal hides to turn them into leather.

thane A Saxon landowner or lord.

thralls The lowest class of people in Saxon times, who were basically slaves.

whey The watery part left when milk is churned to make cheese.

Activities

pp4–5 Raiders

- Use the Internet to find extracts from a Saxon book called *The Anglo-Saxon Chronicle*. Write down any descriptions that tell you how the Saxons felt about the Viking raids.
- Use an atlas and look up the countries of Scandinavia (Norway, Sweden and Denmark). Make your own map of Viking lands, marking on these countries as well as England. Decorate the North Sea with pictures of Viking longships.

pp6–7 A Viking Town

- Write a guidebook about the Viking town of Jorvik, to help a Saxon visitor from the countryside.
- Make a poster advertising the goods the leather-worker makes. Add the prices in weights of silver, for example 5 grams of silver.

pp8–9 Craftworkers and Traders

- Write a short play about a Viking leather-worker travelling around York, trading for the goods he needs from the other craftworkers. Make up some dialogue for each craftworker in which they boast about the goods they make.
- Imagine you are a Viking child who has spent a week watching merchant ships arrive in York. Write a diary, describing the amazing goods you have seen arrive in your town.

pp10–11 Houses and Homes

- Use the descriptions in this book and other books about the Saxons to draw a plan of a Saxon village. Label the hall and houses, and give the village a Saxon name.
- Draw a plan of a Saxon house. Draw and label everything you would find inside.

pp12–13 Village Life

- Make a timetable for a day in the life of a Saxon child. Write down the different tasks for different times of day. Think about what time of year it is and how this might affect the jobs that need to be done.
- Write a short play about a stranger arriving in a Saxon village. Try to think what exciting news they might bring about the king or the Vikings, and how people in the village might react.

pp14–15 Clothing

- Imagine that they had magazines in Saxon times. Write a fashion article describing the latest jewellery to arrive from Scandinavia.
- Design a set of clothes for a Saxon family. Base it on the photographs in the book but add your own ideas. Label the designs with the names of different items.

pp16–17 Food and Drink

- Design and write a menu for a Saxon or Viking feast. Use the foods described in this book and any others you can find in books or on the Internet.
- Look in a cookery book for a recipe for your favourite dish. Now write a Saxon version, using only the food and cooking methods that were available at the time.

pp18–19 Feasts

- Design an invitation from a *thane* to his *churls*, inviting them to attend a feast. What attractions might be described? Who might not be invited?
- Invent your own boardgame called 'Saxons and Vikings', using a chessboard, dice and draughts. Write down the object of the game and the rules.

pp20–21 Storytelling

- Search for *Beowulf* on the Internet and read a part of one of the translations of this amazing story. Then write your own Saxon story, including a hero, a monster and a dragon.
- Pretend that you are a Viking storyteller, and try your hand at 'kenning'. Think of short, poetic phrases that you can use to describe things in your classroom without using their names. For example, a blackboard rubber might become an 'eater of chalk'. Then try 'kenning' to describe other things.

pp22–23 Law and Order

- Use the library and the Internet to find out about different Saxon and Viking laws. Write a list of your ten most important laws and the punishments for breaking them.
- Write a short play describing a trial by ordeal. Remember that most of the characters believe that this is a fair type of trial because of their religious beliefs.

pp24–25 War

- Using a long roll of paper, make a poster showing a Viking or Saxon sword. Use the library or Internet to find pictures of runes, and copy these on to the blade of the sword. Give your sword a name, and write a caption describing the magical power of runes.
- Imagine that you are a Saxon warrior who has just fought against Viking raiders for the first time. Write a letter to your king describing the terrifying ways in which the Vikings fought.

pp26–27 Religion

- Use an encyclopedia to find out about St Augustine. Imagine that he has just died, and write a short article, called an 'obituary', describing his life.
- Use the library or Internet to find a story about Thor. Then write a play, based on the characters in the story, and act it out. Thor is a god with amazing powers, so you can make the play as unbelievable as you wish!

Finding Out More

Books to Read

British Museum Activity Book: The Anglo-Saxons by John Reeve & Jenny Chattington (British Museum, 1999)

British Museum Activity Book: The Vikings by David M. Wilson (British Museum, 1999)

Heritage: The Vikings in Britain by Robert Hull (Hodder Wayland, 1997)

On the Trail of the Vikings in Britain by Peter Chrisp (Franklin Watts, 1999)

What They Don't Tell You About Anglo-Saxons by Bob Fowke (Hodder Children's Books, 1998)

You Wouldn't Want to be a Viking Explorer by Andrew Langley (Hodder Wayland, 2001)

Places to Visit

JORVIK, Coppergate, York Y01 9WT
A reconstruction of the sights, sounds and smells of Viking York.

West Stow Anglo-Saxon Village, Icklingham Road, West Stow, Bury St Edmunds, Suffolk IP28 6HG
A reconstruction of an Anglo-Saxon village on its original site.

Sutton Hoo, Tranmer House, Sutton Hoo, Woodbridge, Suffolk IP12 3DJ
The site of an extraordinary burial mound, in which the grave of an early Saxon king was found, including his treasure, helmet and ship.

Index

Page numbers in **bold** refer
to photographs.